Charlene Fix—in her poems' animal subjects—finds lessons for humanity, though her poems are light, delightful, effervescent, quick-on-their-feet, fleet-footed, with a wit and wonder worthy of Marianne Moore, yet more pendulous (like the dewlaps of a dog) or dew on a spider's web, unfixed and as fleeting as a cicada husk on a flower petal. Fix's humor is earthy, wise, and full of music, the "Music of Voles," for example, that is "in the cremains of owl's fiery furnace, yet singing." The poet knows better, but allows her butcher to say: "Those/ slabs of muscle are but/ empty clothes from which/ the lives have fled." So much looking, so much care, that to inhabit Fix's world is to feel gravity of world always—the tragedy, the immensity, beauty, but to do so—most often, locally, on the dining room table, to see the power of one's "own oats," recognizing father and step-son and son and daughters and dog, and that horse over there, that lamb in the barn at the fair, it's humanness, as noted by a sister. One might say these show family values uncorrupted by the conservative abuse of that term—family values as expressed by a seen-it-all country doctor, or farm vet, or a lighter-lined, slightly quieter Whitman. In Fix, then, we have a poet with a cinematographer's eye—an artist who lights, colors, frames and records the visual with lyrical chains of words in place of celluloid images. As with the best cinematographers, her lenses are well ground and polished; her gaze attentive, careful, and intimate; and she sees more than what is visible. In this gentle and humorous volume, Fix goes beyond her animal subjects as representative to each creature's self and tells their inherent stories. Too often with literature the animal hat is donned in service to the human beneath it, but here in these humble, generous lines even the ghost of a flea reminds us "Surprise! Surprise! The flea is thee."

—Joshua Butts, author of *New the Lost Coast*;
Lesley Jenike, author of *Holy Island*;
and Ariana-Sophia Kartsonis, author of *The Rub*

Other Books by Charlene Fix

Prose:

"The Lost Father in *Death of a Salesman*" (*Michigan Quarterly Review*)

"*Yes!* and *Yass:* Dean Moriarty's Ecstatic and Lugubrious Affirmations in Jack Kerouac's *On the Road* (*Xavier Review*),

Harpo Marx as Trickster (McFarland 2013)

Poetry:

Flowering Bruno: a Dography (XOXOX Press 2006)

Mischief (chapbook, Pudding House, 2003)

Charlene Fix: Greatest Hits (chapbook, Kattywompus, 2012)

Frankenstein's Flowers (CW Books 2014)

Bottom Dog Press

Huron, Ohio

Taking a Walk
in My Animal Hat

Charlene Fix

I am his Highness's dog at Kew;
Pray tell me, sir, whose dog are you?
Alexander Pope, 1738

For Robin/Dave
with love for
animals,
Charlene Fix

Harmony Series
Bottom Dog Press
Huron, Ohio

CREDITS:
General Editor: Larry Smith
Cover & Layout Design: Susanna Sharp-Schwacke
Cover Art: Hannah Ross, www.hannahbessross.com
Author Photo: Christine Kozobarich

ACKNOWLEDGMENTS:

Thanks to the editors of these publications where the following
poems first appeared:

"Dewlaps," *Poetry*. "Horses and Dogs in Old Films" & "The Music of Voles,"
Literary Imagination. "Parable of a Hungry Horse," *The Comstock Review*. "Our
Norwegian," *Red Branch Journal*. "What Dreams May Be," *The Cincinnati Review*.
Republished on the Academy of American Poets Website: https://
www.poets.org/poetsorg/poem/what-dreams-may-be. "Four Cows" &
"Emordnilap," *Forklift Ohio*. "*Country* and *Country*," *Mudfish*. "Kublai Kahn,"
5 A.M. "'Beware the Ides of March,' Says the Squirrel Swept Up in the
Talons of a Hawk," *The Ides of March*, anthology, Columbus Creative
Cooperative. "Colts" & "Choreography of Crows," *Ekphrasis*. "Cats are
Birds," *Antioch Review*. "Leaving the Fair," *Birmingham Poetry Review*. "Sunday
Ducks," *Painted Bride Quarterly*. "Drawing the Gryphon" & "Loitering Geese,"
Heartlands. "Bushman," *Incliner*. "A Bad Sound," *Xavier Review*. "Justin-Juliet
and Sonya," *Crazy River*. "Resurrection," *Pudding Magazine*. "The Same River
Twice" and "Running the Narrative Backwards," *Botticelli Magazine*.

"Sunday Ducks," "The Butcher," "Cats are Birds," "Bushman," "Parable of
a Hungry Horse," and "Resurrection" appeared in *Mischief* (chapbook, Pudding
House Publications 2002). "Dewlaps" appeared in *Charlene Fix: Greatest Hits*
(chapbook, Kattywompus Press, 2012), and *Frankenstein's Flowers* (CW Books,
2014).

CONTENTS

III. *tongue without words*

TAKING A WALK IN MY ANIMAL HAT

I loved it instantly, as sometimes happens when
clothing manifests the state or aspiration of the soul,
in this case a fake fur winter hat with little ears
like a cat's or dog's or bear's. I wear it on walks.
Yesterday, teens in a passing car meowed at me,
then growled and barked. I seized the compliment
and left the chaff. Today a man backed out of a driveway,
honked, and offered not a smirk but a smile of recognition.
This made me feel eccentric, which isn't me, but also
kindred to my dog and cat, and more aware of what
the hair on my arms and legs keeps telling me. In this hat,
it seems possible to detach from the Human Raiders
of Earth positioned in High Places, and to tread
as humbly as the wise and gentle beings in low.

DEDICATION

In memory of the animals who shared our connected lives: Ribby, Arnold Schwarzenhamster, Bruno, Kizzy, Sasha, Rhonda, Sid, Olive, Indira, Ishmael, the Bun, Bonkers, Merlin, Daisy, Taylor, Boo, Lady Brett Ashley, Jessie, Nemmit, and Nellie. And for Harpo, Oscar, Cotton Paw, Marshmallow Paw, Little Ché, Rajah, and Puss, who share them now.

I.

journey through owl

DEWLAPS

I've been fond of dewlaps since
first reading about them in Joyce—
you know, when the young Stephen Dedalus'
father is imitating a hotel keeper by saying,
"He's very moist and watery about the dewlaps,
God bless him," a few pages before he utters
another phrasal marvel, "the Pope's nose,"
to name the butt-flap on the Christmas turkey.
Now I'm growing my own,
a mortal observation of the mystery
of gravity working on meat.

Still, I choose to celebrate dewlaps,
and for this undertaking I select
the extraordinary lobes flanking the mouth
of my sister's one hundred and sixty pound
St. Bernard-Pyrenees mix.

His dewlaps drape his jaws like heavy quilts,
they are twin flags of the Duchy of Dog,
they are hanging exterior files on the cabinet of snout,
they are dueling pendulums of a white-fur metronome,
they are awnings on Dog Hotel
and are thick like a dowager's brocade.

They waft so slowly that they slow
the whole world down. We watch them dance
their damp ballet, and watching, we forget
to watch the troubled world. They fling
a thick white sputum like the ectoplasmic hands
of a clock. So "time is malleable," say the dewlaps.

When the dog they're attached to reclines with a groan,
his dewlaps drape his paws. In fact, they extend
beyond his paws to dampen the floor.
I think someone could hide from all sorts
of obligations under a dewlap.

A few years back I felt an intense hankering

to witness those exceptional flaps. I found myself
singing, "going to see the dewlapped dog,"
and wound my daughter and myself up so much
we braved the January ice, and you can bet
I went down on my bum between "dew"
and "lapped" as I reached the car door.

Nevertheless, today, looking at paintings by Munch
involving curtains and assignations,
I still believe in the possibilities of dewlaps.
Ah Polonius! Perhaps a living arras
would have stopped the sword!

UNTRAINING SASHA

The new dog Sasha rises
on her hind legs, weeping rusty
tears when we return, raking
toenails down our backs
when we hang our coats
or bend to the mail. So we
train her to sit composed,
though we can do nothing
to stop her sentimental tears.
Yet now I'm urging her
to leap and leap again,
for I miss the grand height
she achieved, and I want to
imagine her in a tutu again
as she twirls on oak,
both on and off the little
threadbare Persian rug.

Beyond the beveled glass
leaves are spinning: orange,
gold, and crimson clocks.
There's not enough time
to be good! So I must whoop
her up, chortling names of
everything she loves,
making her dance, and
dancing bestow a solitary lick.

THREE-LEGGED DOG

If wishes were horses, beggars would ride.
If turnips were watches, I'd wear one at my side.
English nursery rhyme recorded 1628

She has four, really lovely ones:
feathered, trousered, skirted, furred—
whatsoever word you use
to name that hair Aeolus-blown—
a look that makes me yearn for fringe
unto eccentricity
(fringe on boots, on jacket, bag).
But one leg doesn't work: she tore
her knee chasing a squirrel. The other
one got fixed by surgery,
but now because her heart's not good
we're hoping rest will rectify
the joint so once again she'll go
for walks and climb the stairs. The jury
may be out on poetry—
if highly compressed utterance
makes anything transpire—but in
my teens, when I grew fearful of
the deaths of parents, bulwarks
between us, reality,
when Ilya Katz's father died,
then Betty Wolf's mother, I prayed
elaborate bargainings and may
have made a horse with wings: my father
rode 'til ninety-four; my mother,
ninety-eight, is still astride,
and that was spoken-word. I lasso
now for no less than the world.
Although the very soulful dog
seems reconciled to eating, napping,
standing silently at doors
for hoists to take a piss, for rides
in car, that magic cave wherein
she rambles far and wide, sniffs air
of distant neighborhoods and fields,
drinks water, munches cookie bones

with no need for exertion, I'm
not reconciled. I want her leg
to mend. I want her back upstairs.
I want our daily walks. I want,
what's more, injustices that clog
the hurting world's machinery
removed, gears primed with oil, so all
who suffer and endure may promptly,
sporting turnip watches, heal.

THE SAME RIVER TWICE

After the deer drowned in the Kokosing River,
a fallen ash forked her above the foam,
limp and elegantly arced like a ballerina.

We watched her from the old railroad bridge
spanning the rising river, our dog straining
as if the deer might yet give chase

and wasn't in the sleep of death so far below.
A week later, debris surrounded her. She'd
swollen, shrunk, and lost her fur. Emptied of panic,

she was the serene queen of the accumulating dam.
For months we forgot her. Then we returned,
when dry July had drunk the river half as wide,

the sunlit dew transforming leaves to jewels.
We couldn't even see her bones. So I'm calling
this *Dead Deer Bridge*, and with hands

likewise snared in the radiant world, I'll lift
her fate above the flow, beyond erasing nature,
what Heraclitus knew, and knows.

RUNNING THE NARRATIVE BACKWARDS

It's not the preferred place to begin,
in this cold and empty field,

clumps of stubborn crabgrass over-munched
and knotted in dirt bickering with scattered rocks,

a solitary outbuilding in the distance.
Yet this is where we enter, circling the path

to the start, which is also the end of the field.
Before today, though not that long ago,

the field was warm and green and filled with muscled steers
in motley coats thundering toward us,

making our dog recoil. You had to walk her off,
but I lingered to absorb their gaze,

for every head in the field was upon me
in mute and mutual comment. Then up the path we went,

I and my escort of steers, their virility dispersed so thoroughly
their grandeur stopped the breath,

an entourage of living meat
divided from me by the dogma of fence.

Country and Country

in memory of Eric

We were taking lots of rides beyond the city then,
past grounded clouds gauzing a heaven of hazy colts,

past mares and meditative cows, and even an occasional
deer grazing wild among them. But you grew confused

when we called this *country*, for you had learned in school
that many *countries* make the world. Yours was America.

How we labored to explain the fullness of the word,
but you folded your six-years' length of arms across your heart,

dismissing us with a skeptical drift of cobalt blue eyes.
You live now way beyond the clouds, in another country

where, at last, we'll all set down our valises full of abstractions
and, like immigrants, take a good look around.

Some will expect winding streets, cafes, and dogs
napping two by two in squares. May they find them.

Others will seek fields of flax and oats, and animals
no hand will ever mar *davening* in fields near open roads,

where deep magenta ironweed shares slopes with orange lilies.

COLTS

after a sculpture by Byron F. Wenger

They lean together, solid, sharing form,
two colts carved from one block of limestone.
They stand on different steppes,
their ears rise up in two uneven sets of points,
but otherwise they're one:
all down their long sides not even air intrudes.
Eight legs, four fused, two gentle V's of chests,
four eyes, closed and Asiatic, two pairs
of nostrils smelling their own skin and fur
and not the world,

                though the world
is implied by their insular joining, just as
the youthful roundness of their bellies gives us age;
their stasis, motion; and this Western urban courtyard, Eastern land.
Strain is whispered likewise in the curve of stone,
the tension of their cleaving.

It's in the line etched between them, in the opposing tilt
of their heads, and beneath their tails that sweep the ground
where the hind legs of one shield a pyramidal point,
the hind legs of the other, seamed mystery.

Yet they are settled at each other's side
in vast terrain that will less likely overwhelm
the two of them than one.

                The sculptor, taking hints
from stone, from memory of easeful bonding in his youth,
has made them to resist the pull of limbs and senses
away from each other and into the world.

CALVES

My calves ache, so I'm walking off the pain in the field

of sleep. It's good to leave the barn to graze with Mother.

Contraction, pull, conflation: we're so close we share

the same wet nurse, her calves, ours, muscled and

growing into brief life, crushing on the redolence

of hay, fur, breath, the warmth of bodies in barns

or herding on fenced grass. Reclining or standing, all but one

face the same way while ignoring what the horses know:

the epiphany that stamps madness on the coinage of their eyes.

The most impressive calves I've ever seen were on a fellow

walking his bicycle through a festival in the park.

They surpassed the width of his thighs, were solid

like the belly of a birthed calf touching down forelegs first,

the cow pleased with the firm flesh she just pushed out

now finding his way to her side, his muscles flexing,

not tearing like ice breaking off from a glacier.

What is passing behind us we can't see. Calves.

THE MUSIC OF VOLES

My daughter has a middle school assignment
that she barely, then she cannot, bring herself to do.
She's to dissect owl pellets harboring undigested remnants of vole.

Let's pause here to imagine furred little lives burning brightly
as they rummage, moonlit, on the forest floor, then eyes like Maglites
guiding a feathered torso to swoop, flat white face looming, hovering still.

She spreads pellets and instructions on the dining room table,
gagging and desperate, then enlists her five-years-younger brother,
who handled bees once with bravado, in the task.

The piano demurs behind them as he pokes pellets,
then tweezes out a few fine and delicate bones, whispers
of vole architecture tarnished by the journey through owl,

slivers in the cremains of owl's fiery furnace, yet singing,
if daughter, son, could bend their ears to hear.

CATS ARE BIRDS

How easily she shifts from cat to bird,
centered on the Oriental rug.
Her feet tucked under rounded feather-fur,
her neckless head a smaller puff that clucks,
she sits upon her nest of secret eggs.
Or when we dine she crouches from the keys,
her front legs arcing like the joints of wings,
her head hung low, a vulture seeking death,
surveying her ancient enemies laid out,
the pig or fowl or fish that hum from plates.
Perched upon the couch's arms, aloof,
she listens to our banter with round eyes;
her ears are tufts of feathers pointing up;
her head ticks to the right; she blinks
disdain like from a tree at night.
Her coat containing colors of all cats,
she flashes light as if her claws had rent
the curtain barring this from this, or else
as if her tongue had licked the final crumbs
of mackerel and left the gleaming bowl.

KUBLAI KAHN

What they said would happen happened.
I shredded current stories as they dreamed
on newsprint sheets and gave the strips
to one who spent his days running on a wheel,
contemplating how to conquer earth and water
and carve new routes of trade while dynasties
rippled and dimmed in his gut. "Do it," they said,
"and be amazed," which is what Genghis said to Kublai
and Kublai to Marco Polo, psyching one another up
to crack the oyster world. So I did, then left the room,
returning to behold a woven tower. And while he lived,
that hamster did such stately pleasure domes decree
from ribbons cut from time and strife that we
believed we lived in Xanadu and not Columbus.

TRANSLATED

The old woman studied the block from her window,
then emerged from her house wearing a hat

to shield her from the lit and windy world. Even in summer,
a heavy coat stooped her shoulders. Neighbors called her

the Mayor, for when a delivery truck stopped at a house,
she asked to come in to see the new sofa, table, or chair.

Once she descended to our cellar to meet our new furnace.
But sometimes she came across the street just to say hello

to the little boy playing on our front porch, "a kindred spirit,"
she said, for he was always wearing a hat.

Because of his great love for that blue cloth hat, it disintegrated.
First its red and white checked bill fell off, then its black strap

let go of his chin forever while the earflaps and crown thinned,
stretching to cover his expanding head.

He is my son, so I believe this happened as he said:
that one day the old woman turned him into a duck.

On that day, he said, before she changed him back
into a little boy again, he paddled around on the porch.

THE DUCKS WITHIN

What goes on in your mind, Mom? S.F.

The question my daughter asks me
has, in this case, an answer:
ducks: orange bills to paddling feet
and quick quacks: five or six
ducks swimming in a circle
on a small pond, leaderless,
though the one who quacks most
is the *me* me, the others me too
but less vocal, in sync,
placid and paced except when,
muscles amped by circumstance,
they paddle faster, bending
their necks to read the water,
dipping and dousing their heads
to parse the edible, beautiful, strange,
before rising for air, supposing *air*
names this vault's wind. If
they could whistle they'd whistle,
not leaving the pond, circling,
the pond circling, and the pond's pond.

BIRD BERRIES

I can hear my father saying, "don't eat the mulberries,"
even as they summon me to pause beneath a branch.

Berries fall toward my appetite with slatternly ease,
some disappointingly bland, others poignantly, sharply sweet.

"Those are bird berries," he'd say in life,
and indeed I can taste particles of straw in them,

and indeed, robins and a sentry rabbit are watching my incursion
while waiting for me to pass, stained and satisfied, as I will.

But I suspect my father in death approves this tree weeping berries into my
           palm
and is helping me find more berries under leaves,

schooled as he is now in the rhetoric of transformation:
berries into birds soaring and splattering chalky ink,

berries into daughter who by this means swallows flight
even while earth is clasping her feet.

DEPARTURE, POISED ON A FLOWER

for Madeleine

You plucked an empty cicada shell from the base
of the loose and rusty railing to place it on
a huge begonia, coaxing from those bits of nature
something new, *Departure Poised on a Flower*,
then you left for New York. The shell, though dry,
is still not pulverized. It treads the turgid flower:
a flash of orange in a stone pot a shade west
of bees breakfasting at Echinacea Diner.

You altered everything by giving birth. Your daughter
knocks us, tickled, out. And in a minor key you changed
the flower, not to mention the circumference of the flower,
by placing on the pillow of a petal this brittle emptiness
with eerie smile, memory as crisp as paper singing
of an absent singer, hollowed out from shedding songs.

BUTTERFLY MOTH

Monarch, I think, seeing black and pumpkin wings
stirring in a patch of impatiens by the porch, though

in truth I have no name for it, pale eater of petals
flamboyantly winged in this season of sudden frost.

There's a moth at the butterfly's center, color
to ghost attached. It is *not me* but *of me* somehow,

as scientists in slow and musical labs are learning to map,
especially its hybrid nature, feeble ascetic bearing art aloft.

I'll call her *Vision Forcing Retrospective Eyes
to Reconcile Dense Chroma with a Tranquil Heart.*

DOGWOOD

It is finally bearing its fruit
of flowers that mimic
the dazed centers of eyes,

petals early camouflaged as leaves
turning white on the slow-
growing dogwood

my husband planted where our
beloved dog Bruno lay down to die
while I was washing his bedding.

My daughter and I found him
lying on his side. We wailed over his body
like Old Testament crones

until my son, fearing that the next door
little boy would chance upon the rictus,
said, "get a grip and cover him."

We thought his worry strange,
but in the next beat the boy skipped
down his steps and whistled past.

The dogwood hesitates to grow,
they say, because its wood
was used to fashion the cross.

For a decade, ours has shown
this very reticence, nor would it bloom.
But now it has ten flowering eyes,

and once begun, there'll be no stopping it.
For when at last grief sees,
it must weep beauty in the face of death.

OUR NORWEGIAN

A Norwegian lived with us ten years.
He preferred to eat fish—the seas were
arable land to him—but we fed him beef.
Mornings, he'd stand on the porch
as if on the deck of a ship in the company
of sailors, and at night he'd dream of
northern lights under bleached stars.
He tolerated English well for it echoed
his native glottals, breaths, stops, and
interjections. His soul, furrowed with
cliffs and evergreens, leaned. His feet
were used to stony soil and the scrapings
of glaciers, but the best we could offer
his expectations were steps down into
a dense ravine. His land was narrower
than ours and lacked our nuanced population,
yet he lavished love on all the faces here.
Deprived of elk, he let deer awaken in him
an active nostalgia. He dressed Norwegian
mainly in winter, when he wore a coat
dense enough for the Arctic Circle
and took a special interest in the frost-
glazed moon. Then his sleep would beget
more sleep, his snores resembling ice
crashing over fjords, while in summer
he would search the night, suspecting sun.
Habituated to peace, he was puzzled by
the belligerence of our politics: to him,
war was anachronism. In short, we were
too fond of our Norwegian, so we made
him stay with us ten years. In doing this,
we may have kept him from himself,
yet now we are what he had been:
we wait on the porch, fish on our platters,
while our house wrenches free of its foundation
to sail us deeply into our Norwegian's sea.

SUNSET

Tigers are melting all over windows
of western rooms: gold and orange
tiger-ooze shining while the day dies,
a sunset glare that saves us from being
ambushed by the lives inside. We're
seared instead by a vision stranger
and more true: late light's low vehemence
that smears the liquefaction of those paws
on glass. We hear the tigers growling
in the forge of flames, so know
the body's rag-wrapped nakedness,
the truth of burning out, the beauty
of that truth, its singing rage, before
the angle alters and the glass goes grey.

DRAWING THE GRYPHON

at the Cleveland Museum of Art

I, a child, was sent to draw the Gryphon.
It was reclined. I sat beside it on the floor,
fearful of its size, its curving scales,
its sloping eyes with ruts beneath them worn
by tears, its beak's broad arc, its mouth
tucked under like a turtle's drooping gently
at the corners down. An infant mammal—
calf or piglet, lamb—was cradled on
the Gryphon's knee and steadied in the valley
of its back by Gryphon's paw. Father, mother,
both, and baby me? Who would make
a thing so strange? Stunned, my pencil still,
I stared and stared but couldn't draw
the Gryphon, so I drew his leafy ear.

Ellie Learns *Night*

You tuck your arms along your sides for swaddling.
On your back and bathed in infant songs,

you sleep from milk to milk. Come morning
you gaze with glee through the sixth floor window

at pigeons poofed from sky and hydroplaning roof to roof,
at Prospect Park's parades of passing people.

At two, you pull the ripcord, releasing dawn
to day, a picture book to read, lay down, retrieve.

At dusk you fret for the departing day.
And it's no joke, this infant existential grief,

though mollified by lamps and love.
You aren't the only kid to at that hour weep.

Power rolls over you like a wave. You can
walk! run! dance! make words like *duck, hello*!

Even in Brooklyn, maybe most of all in Brooklyn,
an AWOL chicken might cross the road!

You speak an elfin language on the telephone,
words effervescing in flowers bubbling in blossoms

blooming in the garden inside you. Today
you learned to name the thing you still dislike

although you like its progeny, the moon and stars.
You say with satisfaction in the saying of it, *night*.

I Was a Little Animal Then

I was a little animal then,
as I am now. My sister liked
to pet the long hair on my arms

and sometimes twist and tangle it.
Perhaps that's why—younger,
smaller—I pounced.

We were givens to each other:
there when the day began, there
all the way through to the end.

Then another, and another.

We told each other stories
with wind, snow, the sound of water.

Actual water simmered
and cleansed us both.

We grew taller, older, older
through daily palaver,

had little ones: sweet, plump,
furry, of our own.

They grew, and were gone.

We viewed our separate
portions of the sky,
unaware of being

freshened and refreshed
by the cold moon,

salted and devoured
by hot stars.

II.

the vexed wind

A Parable of a Hungry Horse

my father's story

On Sundays the horse didn't eat.
It was my day to feed him
and I was afraid. I'd enter the Maine barn early,
trying to pocket my balled-up fear.
His roan head would turn, one thick-lashed
horse eye looking back at me, sad.

Because I was ashamed of being afraid,
I let myself be sent each Sunday
to drag the sack of feed within a yard
of what I knew was there
even if I shut the door against the lemon light:
big square teeth and twitching flanks,
the peril of hooves.

So I'd lean the sack in a corner
and whistle off to breakfast hoping that later,
stoked with my own oats,
I'd be stronger and more brave.
But I wouldn't be, so Sundays grew
distended with his hunger.

Although I'm old, the horse still
gazes at me through the years.
I carry an image,
like a photographer's glass plate,
anxiously: our moist eyes,
our nostrils smoking in the cold barn.

This is my atonement for the horse's
Sunday hunger and my fear.

Leaving the Fair

We amble through the sheep barn, leaving the fair.
The sheep lie gentle, penned and cloaked against the dusty air,
scrubbed white (or black or gray) for judging.

When one rises and bends to nibble hay, my sister starts to say
how human its vagina looks, then begins to bray
against those rumored men who'd force rear hooves into their boots

more easily to take them. I marvel at the modes of exploitation:
this, the veined udders of cows, the cultivation
of flesh between pigs' corkscrew tails and pulsing noses.

Yet as we pass a lamb tethered in its pen, I don't atone
for the chop I grilled the other night and savored down to the bone.
And I think of the sheepherder, lonely with flock in the hills.

Here are some sheep in the fullness of life, lined up for judging.
Here are some tethered for shaving. They're baaing.
Here is a child pushing her lamb with a stick to keep it moving.

I like this barn. I must be reconciled to something dark.
As we walk to the street where the car is parked
my twelve year old son and nephew flank me, talking at once

about the safe-sex promo, the bowls filled with condoms
while telling me about girls on the school bus who use them,
of the friend who found three in a bag on the street and abused them,

of the neighbor who filled one with milk, then stapled it to a tree,
of the long rolls of them at the Soussey Market next to the beers,
each holding one of my arms, singing about condoms in my ears.

THE DEMIURGE'S BOTCH

Either the cat punted it
to make a deranged field goal,
or the struggle inside skittered
the sticky trap across the floor,
so when I stumbled dreaming to the fridge,
I got a breakfast conundrum as profound as Job's.

I stooped to pick it up, screamed
to see a face, fur, pulse, then dropped it fast.

Unable to do nothing, though, I made myself
examine the mouse inside, badly stuck, yet
so ambitious for life he was trying
to leave his foot behind.

On front steps, with butter knife
and tears, I opened up the charnel house,
poured warm suds, then worked the silver
underneath the mouse until it scurried off,
dragging expendable pink and kindred toes.

All the while our cat gazed, robin-sung
and bored, in pleasant light.
"Shall I howl?" I asked myself.
I answered, "yes."

THE SORROWS OF GOD

Sometimes I'd feel sad, seeing my children at meals,
especially when they were very young, in high chairs,

their spatulate fingers lifting syllables of fruit from the tray,
their lips smacking as they looked around, eyebrows raised,

because our jobs, rapport, and sanity
were the scaffolding for all their giggles and glee.

When they were small, seeing them thus with food,
I knew happenstance and the sorrows of God.

Even now, watching the elderly carefully chewing,
I feel the same sea of empathy rising.

We are machines grinding on, craving our fuel:
I with my peanut butter sandwich, my beloved alone at the table,

the cat and dog bending to their bowls,
though I suspect they would fight us for bird or for bone.

I think this and promptly forgive. It wouldn't be plunder.
It is bound we are by love to one another's hunger.

SUNDAY DUCKS

The air is filled with flapping
when ducks like no others descend from the sky,
feathers mottled, faces melted to meanness
by long and blistered beaks.
So this is why our bread and yellow popcorn
couldn't lure the resident ducks—
they heard the portent of this wild swooping
so stayed mid-pond, their heads, necks, chests, wings,
forming arcs of precarious grace.
The invaders slow the water's circles, mount,
and as one does he turns his face to us,
as if by our design his crooked beak,
the blinding sun, the stagnant air,
the oily feathers of his mate.
We lick ice cream and flatten grass
with bare and restless feet, disappointed
that the ducks refuse to follow us to eat,
so watch instead the strange ducks rock
and hammer with their grave distorted beaks
the heads of pretty mates who paddle crayon orange feet,
delivering them to the brutal life
dunked and very nearly drowned.

HOUSE BY THE SEA

We went to see a house for rent on the shore
that was divided from the beach by shrubbery
with sea grass waving in the sandy yard.
It faced the house next door as if too shy
to face full on the sea.

The older couple living on the premises
were renting only the upstairs.
Disappointed, having driven far,
we trounced like trespassers to see.

The ocean's salty breath filled all the rooms
where the extremity of far was near:
the roiling, rolling, foaming, singing sea,
its shiny skin now blue, now green, now white,
until it drank the last of sun and turned to ink.

It would have cooled our heated selves,
our sprouting child, to sleep there, draped
by stars and moon and drifting clouds,
all three of us and that old couple
bundled with the sea.

We didn't rent it though. We didn't want
to traipse through settled lives to come and go,
disrupting measured days of those old manatees

who needed just a little silver more to stay the sea.

STONE FISH

for Eric

You were six when you saw the fossil
fish at *Miscellany*, a boutique floating
on High Street full of exotic things.

You nagged for it intensely, so your tried
and trying Sunday father bought it.
But you couldn't take it home.

That is why we have it still. Clearing
my desk on this first day of sabbatical,
I lift it, seeing your little hand

receiving it from the hand of your father,
old fish swimming in stone, drowning
in stone where it's impossible to breathe,

a fish etched well enough to swim in perpetuity.
Fish! who couldn't save himself or you
but suffered transubstantiation into art,

though Stacey dreamt you in a store
like *Miscellany* where she made selections
from your bounty, and Sonya dreamt you

in a restaurant resplendent with light
where she wept on your shoulder
to have found you there alive.

WOODPECKER

I hear the knell
of the woodpecker
on another sick tree.

Last week I heard it
high in our maple,
pounding.

For years my husband said
that tree is dying,
but I was fooled

by new leaves and
twirling sticky seeds.
Now I see

a third of it is barren.
Upstairs my husband sleeps,
raked by that distant pounding.

His first-born son is sick,
though he doesn't yet look ailing.
Nature will eventually loose

some opportunistic trick
like this woodpecker
steadied by spikes on feathers

seeking meat in the mush of a limb.
His hard beak sounds like
it's firing rivets into a coffin.

ELEGY FOR ERIC

From the cosmetic scraping
that sent you wounded to your maker,
from the sucker-punch of anesthetic
to the Xanax for the shakes, after
years of unilateral parental war
that surely cleft your heart, even
the rituals following your death
felt cold. Formalities after diplomacy:
nothing but good wine, humongous
shrimp, elegant suppers. Where was
the newspaper's black box framing
your face, the list of your feats
and dates, your kin, kindred, next-
of-kin, your fellow spouse published
for all to see? Where was your priest
eulogizing you while drowning us
in incense? Your coffin floating
on the arms of many men? Where
was your cemetery plot with our shod
pigeon-toes around it, not to mention
our wings fanning tablespoons
of earth for earth-to-earth, and
our eyes with their teacups of tears?

SPENT BLOSSOMS

I walk too far this morning on my wounded leg,
hoisting it over fallen limbs slick from last night's storm.

A squirrel is sleeping with eternity on the road,
his eyes staring like mine do, asleep in a storm.

A fledgling cardinal stumbles at my feet. Its father
grazes my head three times, once for each of my children's storms.

My husband wants to plant our entire backyard in corn.
I ask him why, even while my teeth itch for some after that storm.

He saw, inside of an hour, a flock of geese heading east
and a flock of geese heading west. They know about storms.

If I pinch off the spent blossoms, the mountain bluets may bloom again.
Spellcheck wants to change my name to *Charnel* as if I perished in the storm.

THE OTHER SIDE OF LOVE

after Audubon's Birds of America

Rising from the page into an open field,
Brown Thrasher warms round notes in his throat,
Trumpeter Swan hooks backwards for a butterfly.
The artist loved them, so he shot them dead.

Bald Eagle's soliloquy? Swirling tongued complaint.
Arctic Tern's dive? Unnatural twist.
Pelican's Eye? Forever sober light.
Doves and Warblers made to mimic walking hunched in grass.
Sparrows, Jays, with arced-with-wire wings.
Hawk menaces Rabbit,
but who sees the hand that menaces Hawk?
All the while the water looks like silk.

Carrion, berries, bugs, he'd have us think,
unhinged their beaks. But it was he
with his conserving love
that killed them, opened them,
then splayed their star-like feet.

Birds Hitting Glass

We were renting a honeymoon house with new carpet and appliances
owned by a bride who had been abandoned by her groom after falling ill.

Maybe that was why it always seemed like autumn there. The scaly feet
of birds flying the wooded acres hinted at something unseemly

hidden in feathers. We were young. Our baby's internal universe
was expanding exponentially. But the trees were perpetually

sloughing their leaves, and the tomatoes and peppers we planted
in the newlyweds' sandy soil thrust red and green hearts at us

like bribes against the frost. I didn't think *Saint Francis* then,
but I'd see you with birds circling and landing at your feet

through the window facing west. It flamed at five o'clock,
so we shuttered it from within, unintentionally causing reflection.

How could the birds know to fear the doppelgänger sky
with themselves soaring in it? We'd be startled by a *whump*.

Sometimes a stunned bird rose, perplexed, and flew away.
Sometimes one lay motionless beneath the sill.

For the window lied. The husband lied when he bespoke his vows.
We tried not to lie, but the truths we told each other hurt,

though not as wretchedly as glass pretending to be sky.

CHOREOGRAPHY OF CROWS

after Points of Departure II: Nijinsky Variations by Peter Milton

Something is wrong with gravity
and time here. Dancers are bending
their arms to crawl away.

Others are leaping suspiciously high
from the stage below, its depth extreme.
A member of the audience steps off

the seventh tier, floating. Wind
is blowing old man Degas' hair.
Ghosts are clinging to railings

while fugitives from earlier eras
emerge from behind pillars.
Even the crows conspire. Look:

their wings spread over the lights,
shadows cut loose from form.
One, the shadow of a shadow, is white.

"Beware the Ides of March," Says the Squirrel

His tail is waving farewell like the tail of a kite
settling into a current when there's no holding it back—

he's on his way, little camera eyes recording
a sweeping aerial shot, an establishing shot of spring—

forsythia fattening dooryards with butter flames,
ash trees whitening like bleached paper.

Inside the terror of the squirrel's happenstance proximity
to the hawk's predatory and awakened appetite

is silence, like that between breaths at oval tables
where peace blooms after the hammering out.

For the hawk's feathered talons are gripping the squirrel's furred belly
so securely he knows he cannot fall,

and both accepted this moment back when their first cells
were reduplicating, the squirrel agreeing

to be a squirrel in the little-pear-womb of his chattering mother,
the hawk agreeing to be a hawk inside the precarious egg.

But I, kingdomed, phylumed, haired, and wingless burning,
cannot assent, so watch their flight with bitter awe.

THE TROUBLE WITH THIS MERCY

The large roach lying on its back
is dancing a recumbent tarantella,
his last expressive offering to the world.
I slide a sheet of paper under him,
easily done, carry him to a window,
lift the screen, set him free. The trouble
with this mercy is that we are on the fourth floor,
there is no ledge, and it's a long way to the grass.

Hours later I see a baby roach no more
than a quarter inch long strolling across the room,
her reflection riding along in the polished wood.
There isn't much food on the floor, no windfall,
just a crumb or two. But consider this: she
survived the vacuum cleaner and the mop today.

THE BUTCHER

Every morning I bleach
my block of wood and sharpen
my cleaver. But don't, please,
call me a murderer. Those
slabs of muscle are but
empty clothes from which
the lives have fled. Like gods,
the beasts are transubstantiated
into soup or stew, and I
into an acolyte. Whose altar
do I serve? When I look, I see
the well-fed children, slow or
swift as doomed herds, pass.

BUSHMAN

Gorilla formerly of the Chicago Zoo, now at the Field Museum

Dear Bushman, I am sorry that
my daughter Madeleine and I
squeezed behind the glass cube
that displays you knuckling
the ground. We were trying
to see your anus, to learn how
tidily the taxidermists frowned.
Indignity atop indignity; you should
be sleeping in the thwarted earth.

A plaque says you were loved:
ten thousand mourners shuffled
past your cage when you were
dying; when you were dead, ten
thousand more. Because in life
you flung shit at your viewers,
who all said, "nicely done." Good
therapist, who knew that guilt
inspires need for degradation.
Wise philosopher, who acted
on the premise, had you not
the people's consciences would grind.
Bold artist, free with medium.
Trappist monk, mute in spare cell.

A photo shows you being young,
your arm draped on the shoulder
of your keeper. You remind me
of my teenage son, which makes me
wonder what you ate for dinner,
whom you loved, and what wild
branches you'd have swung had
you been free with hairy, tenderly
emerging into manhood friends.

GORILLA GRIEF

I wept once for
gorillas murdered
for their hands and feet.
My doctor ordered
a potion. Before
it kicked in I sank
with a tumbling frown
in the magnifying deep,
and there found the
ravaged, the hungry,
the lost and the sick.
I wound my arms
around them, weeping
into water with a
hirsute voluptuosity
I remember only
as *gorilla grief.*

FREEDOM OR FOOD?

To rescue the sky-blue budgie

you must follow the gaze

of the midnight blue cat

all the way from the toppled

cage to the coarse cloth sack

in the kitchen where you'll

find him on a mountain

of seed, whipping his head

from side to side, spitting

shells and muttering.

A BAD SOUND

Late in this end-of-summer
evening, I'm unwinding,
the room cool, the bed smooth,
the door closed. Silence.
For a moment I'm on top of everything,
so much so I've even swept
and washed the kitchen floor.
Now I'm reading poems sent me
for review. One leg is already planted
in their world that is lovelier than ours
with its dirt roads and gleaners,
and its man churning out paintings
while suffering and praising, his mind
boiling over in a contemporary way.
My other leg is rising to step in too
when I hear a bad sound outside,
a *thump* of heaviness hitting
something like a paved road
that almost doesn't, then does
give a little, the Inscrutable colliding
with the Ineffable, and the latter
absorbing the blow, the resulting
waves rippling out forever. So
I step outside in my nightgown
to see what I can see, the sidewalk
damp on my bare feet, clouds
masking the moon and stars, and
our cat adjudicating these mysteries
from behind the screen door.

Downward Facing Dog

When I practice that *asana*,
which is more than once a day,
especially when the morning sun ignites my inner chlorophyll,

my green eyes drift to my
hobbled collie-shepherd dog,
for I am stealing her pose while she sprawls in the hall

or on a bolstered bed,
or, bestowing tenderness,
lies parallel to my yoga mat where her heat and fur skim

my exercising arm or leg.
And I can offer her only a two-
iris bouquet as recompense for the stretch she is

no longer able to do
but instead must suffer kinks
until they drown inside her. Oh, but it was glorious to see her

zoom in the yard, leap
into lilies as if they were water,
stand on her hind legs to greet us, and ritually do

downward facing dog,
inspiring the cats to do it too,
our yogi who is teaching us *how*, and *what then*.

COMING HOME

The sea's in the air:
mid-May and already
it's ninety degrees. You
have driven all night
to get home. The hall
light is yellow. It falls
on dark oak: the floor
and the stairs a brown sea.
The paint isn't fresh
and the walls are too bare.
The stairs say *come up*
where there's even less air.

The road home was dark
but a breeze filled the car,
intimation of freedom.

The car rolled out of gear
at the pump, the kids
sleeping inside—your
laughter was swatting
fatality's flies, the attendant
oblivious, stacking stale
donuts for midnight's
raccoon.

You had slept not at all
for a month. Despite this
you took the two youngest
to see Lincoln's bed
and his image in stone
with its halo of pigeons,

then drove in the heat
to the angst-ridden house,
without yet its dog
of love, nonchalance,
to bark your way through
the vexed wind.

III.

tongue without words

WHAT DREAMS MAY BE

In my dreams I'm always hovering
before the evening primroses,

their centers of ruby gold and bent
stalks whispering praise to me.

It's always prelude playing here:
bee edicts echoing down days

stung to silence under gauzy clouds,
slivered moons, and in steam

rising from pollen. My portly
body taxis in repose. I fall

in love. Each night I deeper fall,
my buzzing swarm swaddled

alike in dreams. We are fuzzy
monks deep in contemplation

on mountains of mere wind.
Our feet frizzle in prayer. Nectar

rolls in our mouths like honey
withheld. I am orotund rapture:

that is me to thee, dancing on nothing
substantial, swaying in my stripes on thick air.

THE SOMBER BEAUTY OF INSECTS

for Ross

Our conversation should have taken place in April,
laden as April is with scent and sorrow,
but it happened in March, the air still clean
from the excising blade of winter. Buds and snow
mingled on the brick walk from Beaton Hall, its tile roof
glowing orange in the sinking sun, and for some reason
I was complaining about insects. I thought them too
grotesque to love. But you, with your will to shake things
so the beauty falls to the outside, said insects have a somber loveliness.
I turned on the stair I had started to climb, the parking lot
emptying behind you, and suddenly saw the wild machining
of their shapes, the muted passion of their browns and bottle greens,
their stylized repeating legs, the way they lifted in erratic flight,
and for one moment understood imagination's fingers
scratching for the strange—*light, life, love, form,* yes,
but bent and wired, twisted, replicated, shined like chrome.

THE GHOST OF A FLEA

after William Blake's painting of the same name

I know this guy stalking across the floor
with his basket of blood and skin,
his twin thicknesses of thigh.

Transformed from the spirit of anger and revenge,
he's domesticated here, hair braided,
curtains rippling with stars.

Blake heard the flea confess himself
so offered him to us writ large that we might see.
Surprise! Surprise! The flea is thee.

JUSTIN-JULIET AND SONYA

It's so like you, long lithe daughter
who has dabbled in disaster,
to have wedged pebbles in your baby nose,
to have rubied your lips with nail polish,
to have gotten your calves stuck in your pushed up jeans,
to have tangled your hair in the egg beater
until your head was in the cake batter,
to have set your hair on fire in a candle flame,
yet to have handled with grace a small living thing.

You made a home for your hermit crab
worthy of *Vogue*: found the best plastic tray,
sifted clean sand, made a little round of water,
then lined the sides of his world with paper scenes
of palms, blue sky, and waves.

It's like you to have asked if you could
carry him back to Haiti, like you
to feel burdened being keeper of a thing usurped.
Nevertheless, you shined his new shell
and ran him over carpet, paper, wood to develop his mind.

You shrieked when he molted—
thought he had eaten himself, then spat himself out,
thought a new pink imposter had moved into his shell.
You named him *Justin-Juliet* in faithfulness to any gender.
You gave him a lamp.
Yet now we think he's dead,
although we can't be sure.

You say that hermit crabs slip from their borrowed shells in death
to lean back naked into sand and waves,
but he's still in his shell, clinging or rigor mortised.
We know only that we no longer see the hick curiosity
of his "howdy" waving little lobster claw,
his googly eyes protruding on their sticks.

He sits atop a bookshelf in the hall,
a philosophy text, a conundrum.

We lift him every day. He never moves.
He's moldy, silent, probably smells
(we've sniffed him by degrees so wouldn't know).

When I suggest you bury him,
you say you have to wait for spring to warm the ground,
you'd have to plant a pipe for air.
So it seems even you don't know the difference
between the quick and the dead,
you who seemed wise about justice all along,
who have known catastrophe yet handle life delicately,
you who know that breathing isn't all.

RESURRECTION

One day a turtle the size of a fifty-cent piece
crawled out of the soil at the side of the house
and lumbered by on trunky legs as if this episode
were normal. His pace was nonchalant and elephantly slow,
and like an elephant he swayed his head, puzzling the way
while making for the depths of roses festooning the porch.
We had accidentally planted him.

Yet he was emerging like a diner from a sunken restaurant,
or like a plumber who has finished fiddling with cellar pipes,
or like a weary traveler from a far distance, *from China*
we'd have thought, since we dug and dug in that earth once,
trying to get there. Jade green and jet lagged, he shed dirt
until his paisley markings were jewels.

We'd bought him at the five and ten,
one of a dynasty of turtles we intermittently acquired,
bore him home in a white carton, a quick turtle carry-out,
then forced him to be siblings with the turtle strangers
in the artificial-palm-treed, plastic turtle bowl. Some days,
salmonella being as yet unheard, we'd plug the kitchen sink,
run the water to a lake, and bid the turtles swim.

What was their chance of life? Eventually we'd notice,
lifting one, how the shell would fold at the edges
from the pressure of our thumbs, and underneath
the fading turtle-green we'd see a sickly turtle-yellow sun.

So when a head hung out too far on too slack
a strangely angled neck, as if the mind had lunged
trying to escape the spent coil, what else was there to do
but pluck that death-alive-with-horror from the bowl,
lay the corpse in half a cuff links box, and dig a hole?

But one beneficently boring summer day, while we were sprawled,
chewing long blades of grass near the house, we saw
a turtle come alive again, all jade again, jade green
gaining the yard by grandiose millimeters.
He had survived displacements one, two, three,
and habitation in a virtual world, had paddled weary limbs

in a strange white lake lacking island or shore, been held aloft
by Brobdingnagians and met their gaze, and last,
he had been buried breathing in the east-side Cleveland soil
until fear deliquesced to a sigh, and the sun called.

BEAVERS OF SUMMER

They had to be somewhere with their ebony gloss,
their lake-assessing eyes, but they were hidden from view.

For all our hiking by streams and rivers, for all
the tantalizing hints of them, they didn't appear.

Beaverless, I bowed over bridges, reading their script on water.
Being bereft of them was the habit I wore.

Then suddenly beavers have appeared three times like shooting stars:
first on Olentangy River Road, gnawing bark on a wooded slope

around the bend from Target; second at the state fair exhibit,
two beavers napping side-by-side staged behind a fence

so unable to startle the soul awake; third, today,
near Mohican forest, a nonchalant beaver, audacious and slow,

is crossing the road. He bears himself like a chalice filled
to the brim with beaver mystery and slopping some over the sides.

He erases paw prints with his pancake-turning tail, the dark
flame of him doused in the shade of the forest he enters.

He draws a line in the road, calls it summer's border,
dares us to drive across.

THE FOX IN THE RAVINE

Buckets of eastern gold wash the morning road
that wraps the rim of the ravine. But where is the fox

my artist neighbor spotted slackening his pace
to stare him down? I've walked here every hour

but have yet to see the fox although I sense the hot coals
at his center shooting ruddy flames of fur,

the yellow spades of oxidation igniting his eyes.
I almost realize what these are for.

The wind is spreading essence of the crackling fox,
the lonely fox whose gait has named a dance

throughout the ravine. Munching rodents, bird's eggs, seeds,
he scans the sky for omens, catching in the net of his gaze

a cranky owl stretching her wondrous wings, perplexed
that they're fused to such a somber body.

She hides her irritation behind a mask of pale face.
I see her too. Yet the fox knows more than I.

His paws can feel spring heaving like a sleeper's chest,
the itch and stretch of prodigal shoots, the sun that's shaving

shadows from the leaves. Everything lays bare his alter life.
Recently I heard a rumor of a mate. So he's not alone,

this fox I cannot see. Together they are roaming the ravine,
dipping heads to drink the creek, climbing hills of shale,

cavorting nights, for night falls in its fullest measure here
where there's no artificial light. Yet the fox can see.

Four Cows

Last night I unzipped my briefcase
stuffed with four banded bundles
of essays. But the heads of four cows
emerged, a thickly furred bovine variety
patiently abiding, not trying to escape,
their bodies shifting slightly, touching
all down the lengths of their sides.
They seemed to be waiting. For what?
My dog, a herder who prefers to nap,
curled up with them inside.

So today I google "four cows,"
seeking their import. I find
photographs of four cows, folks
claiming to own the same four cows,
four cows causing a train wreck,
and four cows wandering into
someone's kitchen, not to mention
medically esoteric and revelatory
tests done on four cows. So it goes.
I click to pages three, then seven,
only to discover how endless this is:
four cows drinking from a river in Sweden,
four missing cows turning up
at the rancher's son's.

My four cows had round eyes
with long lashes, lakes shaded
by willows on a day without wind.

Cow, With Spilled Coffee

We were admiring the framed drawing of the cow
right before I spilled my coffee all over both of us.

It flooded the table, soaked a magazine, cascaded
over the table's edge and onto our jeans, front and back,

and our shoes, right and left, before pooling on the floor.
It's always astonishing how deep, how wide

an accident can be. Over the mess hung the image
of the cow, not a particularly skillful sketch—

I can well imagine art profs condemning it—
yet it had life. It was an insouciant cow,

a long stalk of alfalfa tilting from the corner
of her mouth, suspended dry above our foiled outing.

Earlier we'd hiked hills under clouds that parted
to admit the sun, closed ranks to sprinkle snow.

We live through seasons here. They overlap,
they multiply, as we grow old.

The cow, however, has been saved,
so smiles, as art smiles, on the grave.

B. J. Working

after a painting of an elephant painting by Peter Zokosky

Green leaves say it's summer, as does the keeper lounging in a chair
while his charge, with gentle largeness, takes advantage of the light,
wielding a brush in a snail-curl of trunk before an easel, his eye opaque.

We can see the trees scrubbed white but not the elephant's canvas,
so we cannot know which way appropriation runs. It's possible
that the elephant is painting a portrait of the keeper, who may be

the painter himself: lazy, generous, and inclined to amuse us
with an insight into the artist's ultimate lack of control over those
heart-breaking pots of paint. One's subject inevitably paints oneself.

MEMORY, WITH BLUE PARAKEET

It was my sister's mischief as much as mine
involving our daddy's hairy chest and
our McLuhanesque way around taboo—

parakeet as extension of fingers—for we simply
loved, on a warm Saturday, Daddy in his chair
reading the newspaper with his shirt open,

to coax Petey—our blue parakeet who sometimes
took perplexing rides at 33 rpm on the turntable
or flew through the flowered-curtained room

to feed the bird in the mantel mirror, smearing seeds
on the glass, or lacking seeds, his shit, reverse synecdoche—
we loved to coax Petey from the perch in his cage,

then lower him to Daddy's chest where we watched
his horned feet get tangled in chest hair
while his head bobbed and his beak yanked fake worms,

for he never grew wise to the virtuality.
Daddy didn't move, except to turn pages
while muttering "ouch!" or "here! here!"

LOITERING GEESE

I saw them while I was turning a wide left
at the hour light skims the vast Chemical
Abstracts lawn where concerts are held
summer nights and where I once heard
but couldn't see Harry Belafonte. Today,
under the winter lawn's deciduous trees
blooming with bald dignity, hundreds of geese
are massing, one soul shattered into fragments
of one entity of flight, black necks chic
against brown feathers, gold webbed feet.
They are pausing between the here and hereafter
where the stuff of science gets condensed to a page,
compounded to honk and spit and take the air.
A goose's eye digests a particle of snow.

BREAD TO THE ROAD

On the third day cooped up in the car
on two-lane roads from Cleveland to
the Manitoba prairie's Winnipeg,

our mother's home, the third day inhaling
the reek of rubber, passing through tunnels
and forests of pines, the parents craning

for a vacancy in cabins or motel, my sister and I
sneaked into the backseat the major premise
of our traveling provisions: the loaf of bread,

then rolled the windows slowly down until
we made a gap wide enough to let the slices
pass into the wind. We left a trail, and you

might think that this was naughtiness most sheer,
but ah, the weary birds could see the wheat's
insipid whiteness shine. They landed in a lull

on the continent's long table to mark it with their beaks.
Our little hands were unseen servants of the whim-
driven muse although we had no Hansel-Gretel need.

CLAY

When Mom, Dad, or the childless neighbor gave my sister and me
bars of red, yellow, blue, and green modeling clay asleep in a box
swaddled in cellophane, we woke it up and went to work
at the kitchen table, making turtles, snakes, and bowls of
tiny eggs while Mom washed dishes to the sound of radio
soaps whose characters' occasional slamming of doors

rhymed with the sound of our fists punching the clay
as we grew agitated that the things we made relaxed back
into now grey and lumpen form. Even critters we froze, an hour out
of the arctic winter relinquished their shapes to the room's heat.

So we took to mixing clay with cotton balls, which I don't recommend
because of the nasty texture: sticky yet dry, uncooperative but lacking will,
resistance wedded to hesitation, simultaneously complicated and forlorn,
not fluffy or smooth but clogged like the guts of an infested curmudgeon.

CARTOON

My favorite moment in cartoons,
the one that makes me say *yes!* and *yes!*
is when the critter getting chased steps off the cliff
but keeps running on air,

remaining suspended and fine, fine,
even spry, until, of course, looking down.
Then descent is swift, breathtaking.

Want truth? I, for one, prefer lies,
the imaginative possibilities, the expansiveness,
hope, but mostly the scaffolding of lies.
Not life-sucking lies, not hate-driven
lovers-of-death-and-destruction
politico-military lies, but lies that make

a turf of air, lies that suspend the soul's soles—

for if not for lies, we'd need wings to get the work done,
the kind of work that must be done
way way out on air.

HORSES AND DOGS IN OLD FILMS

"O my love, where are they, where are they going,
. . .I ask, not out of sorrow, but in wonder."
                    Czeslaw Milosz

Because of animals playing
subtle subordinate roles—the hound
who moseys into the parlor *mise en scene*,
lies down near his master's boots
or lays his head on his mistress' tweed-
draped knees, the sleek horse
hard ridden to snorting like a steaming prop—
I lean into the television amazed.
Silver threaded with light still signifies!
To a man—I mean a horse, a dog—
they are no longer, cannot be, alive.
Include the wayside cows, the chickens
bobbing crested heads, the cats and pigs,
though mostly for most frequently
the horses, dogs, their tender faces, hair,
their air, the wattage of their eyes.
They aren't skeletons exhumed for one more dance—
this isn't The Day of the Dead. It's film!
Neighers, sayers strutting most assuredly
alive under the sway of cellulose,
memento mori packed with paradox:
they will, they do, abide.

ALMODOVAR'S MUSCLED STAG

is tossing his enormous rack, running. Passengers on
his side of the train are watching him through the windows

while those of us in the theater get to gaze both inside
and beyond the train where our camera eyes explore a dusk

dense with the stag's billowing breath. He races in
a John Henry kind of way, a living being competing with,

surpassing in magnificence, a powerful machine.
He senses a mate he cannot reach without penetrating

the train, so seeks a gap while goading, showing up
the train, snorting at his reflection superimposed

on the faces that move with the windows, breaths caught
in their throats. We see the sway of the procreant urge

compelling the stag, his desire mirrored by the double-
riding lovers who join so profoundly they make a daughter

grow even while his vanishing hooves leap beyond
the tracks at the end of the train unseen. The currency

of his lust inserted into them like coins makes them move
as their lives intertwine, then gathers our eyes to the rest

of *Julieta* unreeling, Almodovar's vision of the stag entering us
as a lover might, thrilling and begetting: what cinematic images do.

FAWN'S GAZE

The fawn was telling me something
when I slowed for him to cross
Glen Road. He gazed over his shoulder
at the mirage of my green car dissolving
past the sunrise boundary of his world.
Our eyes locked, and the falsity of time
demurred. Now I need help translating
the umber eyes of that orphaned fawn
old enough to drink the part of me
that understood and vanish with it
into the woods. The rest can't say.
So I'm cleansing the word *gaze* of its
taint of jargon and passing it to you,
a golden ear of corn, a flaming fern.

Dog Dream

I just woke up from having my dog's dream.
This can happen when you're sleeping in the same bed.
Your heads don't even have to be touching.
I don't know what the implications are for people
sleeping together, but let me tell you—a moment ago
a bee flew into the kitchen and I felt an urge
to snap it from the air with my teeth.

Do you envy flying things? In the dream
my dog—but I was she—was running
on the block where I grew up, in bright sun,
leaping and trying to snatch birds from air,
unable to though it seemed worth the try,
then grabbing a ball and running with it
through yards without fences, tongue without words.

RELAY

"The living dog/ has found the old dog's toy."
                    Jane Hirshfield, "Bones"

Her first hour home, the new dog Sasha
climbed onto the sofa, laid her head on
the chest of the man who felt unready
for another dog, then sashayed outside
to a spot beneath the dooryard lilac bush
to dig up a bone. Stripped of meat,
somewhat fossilized, it must have
been buried in his youth by Bruno, our
ten-years' dog who rarely buried bones.

Once I had a student born after
his brother died in Viet Nam.
Like them, our dogs will never meet.
But Sasha made the hinges on the door
that swings between them creak.

Emordnilap

I am looking for God in my dog
who is sprawled upstairs on the deer
and reed patterned rug. I lie with him,
singing "Little Altar Boy" with corny
substitutions you don't need to hear.
Sometimes I sense a message from God
in the way the evening light droops
with a mood not of doom but surrender,
especially when it washes over my dog,
his head on my lap, a comforting pal
who helps me assimilate the news or
warms me as I turn more fondly, sanely,
to books. He loves them too, inspires them,
he and his kind, devours them as I do, but
with his big and little teeth instead of mind.
Today he selected *Moby Dick* from the shelf,
trotting by with it, head high like a proud horse.
I rescued it. How would the debate sandwiched
between the covers concerning "obtainable felicity,"
so raw, so real, so ripe, that catches Queequeg,
Ishmael, Starbuck, Ahab, the young isolation-
ravished Pip as well as me in its net, all of us
at sea, have gone down? Hints of God are in
the manifest: a pipe, a coffin, nursing whales.
Fast-forward to paws, nose, floppy ears, no tail,
a curiosity that tilts the furry head, fellahin
brown eyes. If God is hidden in my dog, then
He is rough. He rips and leaps and nips, as if
a touch of evil lurks in live, a bit of the devil in lived.
Earth too, for he digs and rolls in it as he does
in its near *emordnilap*, my heart. For he can
be gentle. In the morning he leaps on the bed,
but when I mumble, *it's too early yet*, goes back
to sleep, eventually landing on my ribs, coop
of my affections, making his wolf tongue flow
over my face and blessing it as if he owns me.

DEWLAPS REDUX

in memory of the dewlapped dog

The long and short of it is this:
in nine years Merlin never snarled.
His dewlaps wouldn't let him.
They neutralized aggression, were
his character's keelson. Provoked,
he'd pause, say *rrrrrrrruff*, then
toss his head, a mantel of serenity
falling over his face. Often I remarked
his butleresque demeanor, disapproval
professionally hidden in a blizzard
of white fur, then pulverized like kibble
in his tabled soul. Example: he loved
Daisy, the other white dog in the house.
On the day they toasted their betrothal
with cookie bones, she attacked him
for his. But his dewlaps steadied him.
Those quilted counter-weights attached
to that worst of weapons, the mouth,
were deep pouches filled with *gentillesse*.

ABOUT THE AUTHOR

Charlene Fix grew up on the east side of Cleveland as part of the grand engendering after WWII. She states, "I made mischief with my slightly older sister and the other free range kids who lived in almost every house. Yet the city was mostly segregated, the culture reticent, and some adults had tattooed numbers on their arms, so I grew up feeling urgent about social justice." She credits her third grade teacher, Betty Acker, for starting her writing poems.

Charlene left home for Ohio State, later returning for graduate school. She met her husband during anti-war demonstrations at OSU. She had a stepson and has two daughters and a son. They shared their home with a series of dogs and cats. After not writing for a decade while raising kids, she found herself buying reams of paper, anticipating poems and prose to follow.

Charlene taught high school English for ten years, then was a professor of English at Columbus College of Art and Design for more than thirty. She has received Ohio and Greater Columbus Arts Council grants, two prizes from The Poetry Society of America, and her poems have appeared in various literary magazines. She wrote a study of Harpo Marx in the thirteen Marx Brothers films called *Harpo Marx as Trickster*. Her books of poems are *Frankenstein's Flowers* and *Flowering Bruno: a Dography* (with illustrations by Susan Josephson). Her poetry chapbooks are *Mischief* and *Charlene Fix: Greatest Hits*. Charlene workshops with The House of Toast poets, co-coordinates Hospital Poets at OSU, and is an occasional activist for Middle East peace.

BOOKS BY BOTTOM DOG PRESS

HARMONY SERIES

BOOKS BY BOTTOM DOG PRESS

APPALACHIAN WRITING SERIES
Brown Bottle: A Novel, by Sheldon Lee Compton, 162 pgs, $18
A Small Room with Trouble on My Mind,
by Michael Henson, 164 pgs, $18
Drone String: Poems, by Sherry Cook Stanforth, 92 pgs, $16
Voices from the Appalachian Coalfields, by Mike and Ruth Yarrow, Photos by
Douglas Yarrow, 152 pgs, $17
Wanted: Good Family, by Joseph G. Anthony, 212 pgs, $18
Sky Under the Roof: Poems, by Hilda Downer, 126 pgs, $16
Green-Silver and Silent: Poems, by Marc Harshman, 90 pgs, $16
The Homegoing: A Novel, by Michael Olin-Hitt, 180 pgs, $18
*She Who Is Like a Mare: Poems of Mary Breckinridge and
the Frontier Nursing Service,* by Karen Kotrba, 96 pgs, $16
Smoke: Poems, by Jeanne Bryner, 96 pgs, $16
Broken Collar: A Novel, by Ron Mitchell, 234 pgs, $18
The Pattern Maker's Daughter: Poems,
by Sandee Gertz Umbach, 90 pgs, $16
The Free Farm: A Novel, by Larry Smith, 306 pgs, $18
Sinners of Sanction County: Stories, by Charles Dodd White, 160 pgs, $17
Learning How: Stories, Yarns & Tales, by Richard Hague, $18
The Long River Home: A Novel, by Larry Smith,
230 pgs, cloth $22; paper $16
Eclipse: Stories, by Jeanne Bryner, 150 pgs, $16

Bottom Dog Press, Inc.
P.O. Box 425 / Huron, Ohio 44839
http://smithdocs.net

CPSIA information can be obtained
at www.ICGtesting.com
Printed in the USA
FFOW02n1234080718
47317946-50320FF